I am dedicating this program to my daughter and every child in the world who's affected by Bullying or Abuse:

Sian Williams

a.k.a
The Kidzucate Kid

Life is full of challenges and yours started very early in life. Through your stutter you taught me that you are never too young or to old to make a difference. Your fight to help others is an inspiration to children and adults all around the world.

With all my love!!!
Mum

"In a gentle way, you can shake the world."
~Mahatma Gandhi~

Copyright & Disclaimer

2018 Azelene Williams

All rights reserved. No part of this book may be reproduced, stored in a retrieval system or transmitted in any form by any means without the prior written permission of the publisher, except by a reviewer who may quote brief passages in a review to be printed in a newspaper, magazine, or journal.

First Publication 2016, Second Publication 2017, Revised Publication 2018

DISCLAIMER

While Kidzucate makes every effort to ensure that all advocacy and program material on this site is accurate, of high quality and up to date, such material does in no way constitute the provision of professional advice. Kidzucate does not guarantee and accepts no legal liability whatsoever arising from anyone purchasing any advocacy and program material contained on our website or any linked site or person. This includes advocacy and program material that is sponsored by Kidzucate from time to time as well. Users should seek appropriate independent professional advice and insurance before purchasing any advocacy or program material available for purchase on our website or any other linked site or person.

Melbourne   **New York**   **London**

Printed in: **Australia, the United States of America and the United Kingdom**

About Us

Sian Williams
Founder of Kidzucate

In 2013, at 6 years of age, Sian Williams founded Kidzucate. Also known as "The Kidzucate Kid", Sian felt inspired to start Kidzucate when she suffered bullying at school because of her stutter. Sian refused to become another statistic of bullying and found a fun, kid-friendly solution to her problem.

Kidzucate kicked off with Sian using YouTube to present her educational videos, teaching kids how to be better kids. Sian's vision was to not just talk about bullying, but to mentor children her age as she believed kids learn better through kids. When Sian is inspired, she speaks out through her YouTube videos and gives tips and advice on things which have happened in her and her friends' lives. Sian's initiative has a huge impact on other children. They can relate to the issues raised by Sian and respond positively towards her work and mission.

Sian also inspires adults, receiving more and more acknowledgment and support from diverse media outlets and recognition through awards both nationally and internationally.

In 2014, Sian was invited by the Youth for Human Rights to attend their Youth Summit in Brussels, Belgium to represent Australia. She was the youngest delegate in the world to attend the Summit. She was awarded the Human Rights Hero Award – at age 7 she was the youngest person to ever receive this prestigious award. Sian gave a 15-minute speech to the audience of 300 people.

Other awards Sian has achieved include:
2013 **Citizenship Award** - for Quinns Baptist College – Age 7.
2014 **International Human Rights Hero Award** - In Brussels – Age 7.
2014 **Pride of Australia Young Leader Medal** - for WA – Age 7.
2017 **Governor's City of Joondalup Youth Citizen of the Year Award** – Age 10.
2017 **House Counsellor for Windsor** - for Lake Joondalup Baptist College - Age 10.
2017 **High Achievement Award** - Lake Joondalup Baptist College - Age 10.
2017 **Civics & Citizenship Award** - Lake Joondalup Baptist College - Age 10.
2017 **City of Joondalup Student Citizenship Award** - Age 10.
2018 **Head Girl** for Lake Joondalup Baptist College - Age 11.
To receive these awards at such a young age is a truly outstanding achievement.

About Us

Azelene Williams
Co-Founder of Kidzucate

In addition to being a wife and mother, Azelene Williams (Dip. Holistic Counselling, Dip. Community Services Work, Cert. Domestic and Family Violence, Cert. Sexual Intelligence) is currently furthering her studies with a Bachelor of Social Work through ECU.

Azelene is a confident, intensely motivated as well as an experienced businesswoman and social activist. As a Qualified Holistic Counsellor, Published Author, Chief Executive Officer and Co-founder of Kidzucate, Azelene pursues her passion for Social Justice and other Women & Youth issues.

Originally from South Africa, Azelene has also lived in the Middle East before settling in Perth, Western Australia in 2011. Her passion to empower women all over the world was inspired by her own personal traumatic experiences which are documented in her two books INFERTILITY Road to Hell and Back (ISBN-978-0-646- 57555-1) and BROKEN Breaking the Silence (ISBN -978-0-646-94545-3).

Azelene personally experienced three and a half years of physical and emotional abuse as a teenager in her first relationship. She came out a stronger person and now teaches youth and adults about unhealthy relationships, how to identify them and how to safely break free from them. Her life's ambition as an activist in the field of domestic and family violence is to have a positive impact both on today's and future generations.

Azelene has proven successful in developing strong, trusted relationships with individuals from diverse age groups, organisational levels, cultural heritages and socio-economic backgrounds by combining exceptional communication, interpersonal and mediation skills with industry-leading therapeutic methodologies. When you combine the determination of a young stutterer who refuses to let bullies get her down with a mother's fight for justice, the result is a winning pair with a drive to help make the world a better place.

Take-A-Stand
Harm Prevention & Healthy Behaviour Development Program

"Kids learn better through kids"

Our **Vision** is to create a happier world for our children and youth.

Our **Mission** is to empower young people with the knowledge and awareness to identify child and youth related issues and take appropriate action towards their own and other children's safety and wellbeing.

Our **Objective** is to promote the prevention or the control of behaviours that are harmful or abusive to human beings, primarily in emotional abuse, physical abuse, sexual abuse and substance abuse. Our objective is carried out through our peer-based programs.

INTRODUCTION & RULES

The **Kidzucate Take-A-Stand – Healthy Behaviours Development Program** has been created to teach specific interpersonal skills to children and their parents. This is a Kids Workbook a tool to build resilience it is not a Professional Training Manual. For professional training refer to our website www.Kidzucate.com

Rules when using this book:

- Remember this Child Workbook is just a tool to build resilience, you can use the worksheets in any way you want.
- Being an Advocate and using your Peer-based Child Workbook does not make you a trainer.
- Have fun when sharing the peer-based ideas and concepts you have learned in this book, but make sure you always get a trusted adults permission to use these concepts in the community.
- Always make sure you are safe and never intervene in situations that are dangerous.
- Always seek help from a responsible adult to assist you.
- Always get permission from a responsible adult when you want to Advocate against Bullying.
- Always get permission if you want to distribute Advocacy material at your school, community, and other places. Don't just go ahead and do so without permission.
- Kidzucate does not take any public liability when you use the tools, ideas and concepts in our programs. Also see our disclaimer on page 2.

 Videos are available for these topics

  Page number in Child Workbook

  Page number in Teachers Manual

Adult Role in Prevention of Bullying

As soon as children begin to interact with others, we can begin to teach them not to be bullies and not to be bullied. We can give them words for their feelings, limit and change their behaviours, and teach them better ways to express their feelings and wishes. **Children do not learn to solve these kinds of problems and get along by themselves. We need to teach them.**

When preschoolers begin to call people names or use unkind words, intervene immediately and consistently. In kindergarten, children learn the power of exclusion. We begin to hear things like, "She's not my friend and she can't come to my party." Respond with, "You don't have to be friends with her today, but it's not right to make her feel bad by telling her she can't come to your party."

In the early years, cliques and little groups develop which can be quite exclusionary and cruel. Children need to hear clearly from us, "It's not right to treat other people this way. How do you think she feels being told she can't play with you?" Kids don't have to play with everyone or even like everyone, but they can't be cruel about excluding others.

Boys who are physically small or not as strong are more prone to victimisation. Making fun of, being picked on and other forms of bullying need to be identified in their earliest stages. The message needs to be crystal clear. "This is not okay. Think about how he must feel. How could you include him and let other kids know it's not right to treat others this way?"

Children who are not bullies or victims have a powerful role to play in shaping the behaviours of other children. **Teach children to speak up on behalf of children being bullied.** "Don't treat her that way, it's not nice." "Hitting is not a good way to solve problems, let's find a teacher and talk about what happened."

While the Take A Stand Program methodically introduces concepts and skills that are age appropriate and can be used daily as children learn to address interpersonal conflict more effectively, adult intervention and guidance is an important element.

Intervention With Children that Bully

Children who bully need to be dealt with consistently and effectively. Bullying should not be overlooked or excused. We know bullying behaviours only escalate as children get older and the ramifications for children that bully and the group as a whole are significant.

DO NOT BLAME. Do not get into a discussion about the "whys" of what happened. Your discussion with a bullying child should focus on several key points:

Bullying is not acceptable in our school, family or in society.

If you are feeling frustrated or angry or aggressive, here are some things you can do. Then provide concrete examples based on the current situation.

Role-play or act out the new behaviours so your teaching is experiential. Remember that role-play is the key to changing behaviours!

Ask, how can I help you with this? Who could you go to in school if you see yourself getting into this type of situation again?

Specify concretely the consequences if the aggression or bullying continue. Your objective is to stop the behaviour, understand the child's feelings, then teach and reward more appropriate behaviour.

What Happens Inside my Body when I get Bullied?

- ❖ In my Head - _____
- ❖ In my Neck - _____
- ❖ In my Chest - _____
- ❖ In my Heart - _____
- ❖ In my Arms - _____
- ❖ In my Tummy - _____
- ❖ In my Legs - _____
- ❖ In my Feet - _____

Make a list of things that happen inside your body when you are Bullied. How does it make you feel?

Explain in your Own Words what you Think Bullying is

_____

_____

_____

_____

_____

_____

What is Bullying?

Bullying is **repeated** physical, or emotional aggressive behaviours by a person or a group towards a less powerful person or group that is intended to cause harm, distress or fear.

Why do you Think Kids Bully?

_____

_____

_____

_____

_____

_____

Why do Kids Bully?

- They might be attention seekers.
- They might be threatened by the child they Bully because:
    - The child might be doing better in school, at sports or have a happy family.
- They might think being a Bully will make them popular.
- Most Bullies think they are important when they Bully.
- Poor supervision and discipline at home and school.
- Lack of rules at home or school.
- Children that Bully might have uninvolved parents.
- They might be uneducated and don't understand that everybody isn't the same.
- Some children that Bully others, come from families where everyone is angry and shouting all the time. Growing up that way can be very hard and that might be the reason for a child to act out what they have learned at home. They might even think acting that way is normal.

Common Types of Bullying

(Cyber Bullying is more common for teens, but research shows that cyber Bullying can effect any child from as young as 9 years old or as soon as a child starts using the internet and visiting social media sites and pages)

Circle the ones you don't understand – we will look at their meanings later.

Physical	Verbal	Emotional	Group	Cyber
Hitting	Name Calling	Exclusion	Peer Pressure	Exclusion
Pushing	Teasing	Talking About	Excluding	Flaming
Kicking	Being Mean	Acting Superior	Making Fun	Outing
Shoving	Making Fun	Being Mean	Taunting	Trickery/Phishing
Pinching	Bad Language	Not Caring	Set Up	Harassment
Violence	Verbal Abuse	No Conscience	Threats	Impersonation
Physical Abuse	Bossy	Thoughtless	Gang Up	Denigration
Destructive	Shouting	Gossip	Name Calling	E-mail & Text
Spitting	Taunting	Threatening	Pranks	Videos & Images
Tripping	Cursing	Belittling	Gossip	

Make a **X** next to the Bullying you have experienced before.
Make a **O** around the word you do not understand.

What is not Bullying?

Bullying is not one of the listed types we just looked at, if it happened accidentally or if it was a one off !!!!!

Remember all children make mistakes. But it does NOT make them a Bully for slipping up once or twice! We should rather try to understand why they act the way they do before we label them as a Bully!

Question Time?

Have you seen Bullying happening in your school? Please explain.
_____
_____

Have you ever been Bullied before?
_____
_____

Which of the behaviours that we've listed have you seen before?
_____

Things you can do when you are Being Bullied:

* Ignore the person who Bullies you and look for help.
* Report it immediately.
* Say: "I am not scared of you, and I will report you".
* If they make fun of you, smile and walk away.

* Walk away as soon as the Bully approaches you.
* Shout Out: "STOP" – and walk away.
* Go play or sit with someone else.
* Try to avoid sitting or walking alone.

List 3 More Things you can do when you are being Bullied:

1._____

_____

2._____

_____

3._____

_____

How Does it Feel to get Bullied?

_____
_____
_____
_____

Make a **X** in the box to explain the feeling you associate with Bullying! Then explain why in your own words.

30 19

Here is Some of the Feelings you might Experience when you are being Bullied:

Angry	Sad	Weak
Dreadful	Embarrassed	Stupid
Dumb	Hurt	Silly
Nervous	Scared	Hating
Horrified	Devastated	Mad
Grumpy	Depressed	Alone
Frustrated	Overwhelmed	Terrible

Make a **O** around the feelings you have experienced before.

Question Time

Is it normal to feel this way when you are Bullied? _____

Do you have a right to talk to somebody about this? _____

What if the Bully threatens you, are you still going to tell?
_____

Who can you talk to about what happened? _____

_____

What is Communication?

_____

_____

_____

Communication has Three Parts

Words ~ Speak up and say what you mean.

Body Language ~ The way you stand. Stand strong and confident.

Eye Contact ~ Looking somebody in the eye, shows them that you are not scared.

What Does it Mean to be Brave?

We don't always feel brave, but looking and acting brave can make a huge difference. Children who Bully others don't normally target children who are confident and have a strong personality.

Working on your **Words, Body Language** and **Eye Contact** can make a huge difference!

Practice this in front of the mirror often.

Possible Ways to Respond when you are Being Bullied

POSSIBLE RESPONSES
Ask them to stop pushing you.
Leave the toy and go ask for help.
Tell the child that you will report him if he does not stop.
Shout out in a strong voice: "Don't do that, give it back."
"I'm going to tell if you do that again."
Leave the toy and go play with someone else.

How Else can you Respond?

_____

_____

_____

_____

_____

_____

Exploring Different Feelings

What feelings do you experience when you are a Victim of Bullying?	What feelings do you experience when you are the child that Bullies?	What feelings do you experience when you see someone Bullying a child?

Some Feelings you Might have Experienced!

What feelings do you experience when you are a Victim of Bullying?	What feelings do you experience when you are the child that Bullies?	What feelings do you experience when you see someone Bullying a child?
Pain	Powerful / Taking over	Sorry
Want revenge	Superior	Mad / Angry
Shocked	Lonely / Isolated	Confused
Hurt	In Control	Scared / Afraid
Want to Bully back	Tough	Worried / Anxious
Get Bully in trouble	Sad / Depressed	Vulnerable / Uncertain
Alone	Anger	Want to defend person
Embarrassed	Guilty	Dislike / Hatred
Afraid / Terrified	Afraid / Cowardly	Guilty
Sad / Depressed	Mean	Revengeful
Hate	Getting Attention	Sad / Depressed
Angry	Pain	Shocked

Circle the feelings you have experienced before.

Things we are Able to Say and Do When we are Being Bullied

STATEMENT	BEHAVIOURS	ACTION FOR HELP

Things we are Able to Say and Do When we are Being Bullied

STATEMENT	BEHAVIOURS	ACTION FOR HELP
"That wasn't nice"	Walk away	Go play with other kids
"Don't do that"	Join another group	Go and report it
"I'm going to tell if you do that again"	Get away and report the person	Tell an adult you can trust
"That really hurt my feelings"	Ignore them, and walk away	Tell a parent or other family member
"That's not a very nice thing to say"	Act like you don't care	If you are really afraid for your safety, run for help
"Give that back or I will report you"	Avoid the child that Bullies	Scream for help
Make a joke – "Whatever" "No kidding" or "So what"	Pretend you don't care and that it's not bothering you	Keep on reporting it, and don't give up
"Is this how others treat you?"	Make a joke about yourself	

Some Great Comeback Lines

COMEBACK LINES AND STATEMENTS

Whatever, I don't really care about………

I am sure you must feel lots better now about yourself.

If you talk about me behind my back, clearly my life is very interesting to you.

Wow, did you come up with that all by yourself?

Your behaviour is so uncool. If you really want to be cool, I suggest you make some serious changes.

I have no idea why you say these things about me. Not even I believe them.

I am sure deep inside you, you really like me. Why else would you waste your time talking about me.

You are really getting boring, keep it fresh and think of something else to say.

I was hoping that you would notice …………….. Would have been heartbroken if you didn't.

I really hope that one day when you have children they don't experience a child like YOU in their life.

Is this how people treat you? I am here if you want to chat to me about your feelings.

This Program is Called Take-A-Stand

What does **Take-A-Stand** Mean?

When you take a stand you speak out about things you believe in. You do this because you know it is the right thing to do. You are able to look people in the eye and say "No" or "Yes", this is what I stand for and nothing is going to change my mind because I believe in myself and what is right."

My Name: _____

My Age: _____ Today's Date: ___/___/____

Photo of me.

In becoming a Kidzucate Advocate

I, _____ am taking a pledge to **Take-A-Stand** against Bullying and any other form of Harm towards myself and others!!!

The Kidzucate Advocacy Pledge
Let's say this together!

I am Taking-A-Stand to:
- ❖ *Treat people with respect.*
- ❖ *Treat people fairly.*
- ❖ *Respect people for who they are and what they believe in.*
- ❖ *Speak out against Bullying.*
- ❖ *Stand up for my friends and family.*
- ❖ *Say* **NO** *to things that I am forced to do, when I know it is not right or when I don't feel safe.*

I am doing this:
- ❖ *Because I want to live in a happy, safe, friendly community.*
- ❖ *I want to go to school because it is fun to be at school.*
- ❖ *Because this is how I want to be treated.*
- ❖ *Because I would like to teach others about Taking-A-Stand and what it means.*

Do you Know what Advocates Do?

When you stand up for someone else you are an ADVOCATE!

Being an Advocate is:
- ❖ Being a friend.
- ❖ Being a good leader.
- ❖ Helping our school and community to be a place where people are treated with respect and kindness.
- ❖ Advocating against Bullying.
- ❖ Standing up for others in need.
- ❖ Treating people with respect.

"Let's say this together"
An Advocate is.......

An advocate is a person who stands up for others and speaks out for them if they themselves can't do it.

Advocates Take-A-Stand in what they believe in and they are not afraid to voice themselves to help others.

Advocates are confident and know how to communicate and make a positive change through that.

Advocates can be any age!!!

An Advocate's Primary Message Should be……

- ❖ You need to stop that behaviour, what you are doing is not right and it's unacceptable.
- ❖ I do not want to be around somebody who is disrespectful of others and treats people the way you are treating people around you.
- ❖ You do not scare me, and I am going to report your behaviour if this behaviour doesn't stop right now.
- ❖ You need to take responsibility for your actions.

Question Time

How does it feel to be left out or excluded from games?
_____

How does it make you feel when you see someone else being excluded from something?
_____

How does it make you feel to stand up for what you know is right and to be an advocate for somebody else?
_____

Can you only advocate for people you know?
_____

78 38

Is it Tattling when you Report Something that Happened to you or Someone Else?

No, tattling is when you tell on another kid or your brothers or sisters to get them into trouble for no reason at all.

Telling because you need help with a problem is **NEVER** tattling.

NOTE!!!

I'd like you to pay attention to your own behaviour for a few days and see if you can identify times when you are a bit of a Bully or if you see someone Bullying others.
Notice how you feel and how it makes other people feel.

Question Time

Who can tell me about Bully behaviours that they observed at home or at school or on television?

_____

_____

Have any of you ever advocated for someone else? Explain what happened, what you did and said and how you helped in the end.

_____

_____

What other ways have you thought of to respond to Bully behaviours?

_____

_____

Question Time

❖ What about when your efforts aren't enough? _____

_____

❖ When do you think you should go tell an adult you can trust? _____

_____

❖ Have you ever reported Bullying behaviour to an adult? _____

_____

❖ How did you feel about doing that? _____

❖ What happened? _____

❖ If the adult did nothing, how did you feel about that? _____

Activity Time

❖ I have never Bullied anyone? _____
❖ How does that make me feel? _____
❖ Do I ever let myself be Bullied? _____
❖ How does that make me feel? _____
❖ Have I ever seen someone else being Bullied and stood by doing nothing? _____
❖ How did that make me feel? _____
❖ How could I Take-A-Stand to stop Bullying? _____

We all Make Mistakes, but we should Learn out of our Mistakes and Fix Them!

Pay attention to how you treat other people. If you want to be respected, you should learn how to respect others first.

Saying sorry after you've hurt someone else's feelings is not always easy, but.....

Learn to say I am Sorry more often!
It will make a huge difference!

Question Time
Adults and Bullying

❖ Are adults sometimes Bullies or is it just kids that Bully?

_____

❖ Do you think an adult has the right to Bully a child? _____

_____

❖ How do you know when the adults around you are stressed?

_____

Physical Bullying

- Have you ever been punished? _____
- Did you ever feel that the punishment was unfair? _____
- What if someone spanks you so hard that it leaves bruises and marks that are still there the next day, is that right? _____
- Does anybody have the right to punish you like that? _____
- What if they say they only did that because you were bad? Do you think that is right? _____
- Would you be afraid to tell somebody? _____
- Do you have the right to tell an adult you can trust? _____

Important!

You need to know that no child ever deserves to be punished by an adult in a way that leaves marks or bruises that are there the next day.

Telling someone else about what is happening to you is important, so you don't continue to get hurt.

It will take a lot of courage to ask for help in a situation like this, but it is important that you get help when you're not feeling safe at home or in any other adult's care?

Adults are sometimes stressed and that stress can turn into anger towards you. It is important to know the difference between normal and problem anger.

Do grown-ups ever hurt with their words?

Yes, sometimes it does happen. What is important: Just because an adult gets upset and says things that aren't always very nice to hear, doesn't mean they always mean what they say.

It is important to understand and to remember that adults also sometimes mess up, get angry and say things they don't mean. It is also crucial to know the difference between that normal anger outburst and problem anger.

Normal anger can be ok, as long as it doesn't hurt you or anyone else physically, emotionally, sexually, verbally or in any other way or form. Adults also should never make you feel responsible, ashamed, guilty because of what happened. If any of these happen and it makes you feel scared, you need to talk to someone you could trust. These types of behaviours are more problem anger than normal anger.

If an adult gets angry, screams and throws something down but is not hurting you or anyone else, this adult might just need some space to deal with a problem. So exploded anger is not always problem anger. If anything happens and you are not sure, it might still be best to talk to someone you can trust to understand what happened. If you feel safe, you can even ask the angry adult afterwards to explain to you what happened to them so that you understand. Do not leave things that bother you.

Sometimes giving an adult a bit of space will help them to calm down quicker. If it's safe and you can, walk away, and give them the space they need to deal with their situation. That might be just what they need. But if this happens every day it can be a problem. If you think, this is an issue in your life you should always talk to someone you can trust.

Adults Also Make Mistakes

If an adult says to you: "You're so stupid, I can't believe you are my child."

Does that hurt? _____

Is it true just because the adult said that? _____

Of course it is **not true!**

What should you do when this happens? _____

We want you to practice saying **"That's not true about me"** in your head when an adult says something to you that isn't true or not very nice about you and talk to someone you trust about it.

We've talked about speaking up for yourself and intervening when you see other kids in trouble.

But what if you need to get adult help. Who are some of the people who can help you if you have a problem? Who loves you and cares about you?

Who else could you talk to if you were having a problem?

What if you had a problem and you tried to tell someone in your family, but they didn't listen or didn't understand what you were trying to say?

It's important that children learn how to effectively get attention when they need help. Often parents, teachers or other adults are too busy or preoccupied to really listen to what children have to say. Role playing helps children learn appropriate ways to get attention when they need it.

Let's Talk List

If a family member or adult who looks after you hurts you with his or her words and it happens to you a lot, you should talk to someone about it and get help to deal with your feelings. One important benefit of you asking for help is that the adult who is having a hard time can also get help with handling their problems.

If you need to ask for help and it is not such a huge problem but you still feel you can't deal with it alone, who would you talk to?
It is a good thing to have between 1 and 3 people on your Let's Talk List.
These people can be a Friend, Family Member who does not hurt your feelings, Teacher, Sports Coach or anybody who loves and cares for you.

If there are really bad things happening at home or with the person who looks after you and you get physically hurt as well or touched inappropriately by this person, whom can you talk to?
These people are on your IMPORTANT Let's Talk List***! They can be a Parent who you trust, another Family Member who you trust, Police, Teacher, Chaplain, Kids Help Line, Department of Child Protection.***

Do you have a right to tell when somebody emotionally and physically hurts you? _____

Even if the adult says to you don't tell anyone but you believe what is happening isn't right, you should talk to an adult you can trust. Remember you are a child and you are allowed to get help no matter what.

My Let's Talk List

If what happened is not that bad but I still need to tell someone because I don't know how to deal with it, I am allowed to get help and I will talk to:

1._____ Why this person: _____
2._____ Why this person: _____
3._____ Why this person: _____

If someone physically or emotionally hurt me or if someone is touching me inappropriately in any way, I am allowed to tell and I will talk to:

1._____ Why this person: _____
2._____ Why this person: _____
3._____ Why this person: _____

Important Let's Talk Contact List

- ❖ Child Protection and Family Support: 08 9222 2555
- ❖ 1800RESPECT: 1800 737 732
- ❖ Kids Helpline: 1800 55 1800
- ❖ Lifeline: 13 11 14
- ❖ Police: 000
- ❖ WA Child Safety Services: 1300 310 083
- ❖ Commissioner for Children and Young People: 08 6213 2297
- ❖ eSafety Commissioner: 1800 880 176
- ❖ _____
- ❖ _____

Getting Someone's Attention

Getting a person's attention when you need help has to be effective! To pull on their clothes and to put your face in their face to get their attention is more annoying than effective. So let's look at effective ways to get the attention you need:

❖ You can actually get someone's attention by asking for what you need. Use a bold voice and say something like: *"Please stop reading your book and look at me please. I have something very important to tell you."*
❖ If you do that, the person will actually stop what they're doing and look at you.
❖ Remember to use the three elements of communication at all times:
  - Make eye contact.
  - Say exactly what you want to say and make it clear that you have a problem and that you need help.
  - Consistent body language.
❖ Make sure the person understands your problem and does something about the problem or refers you to someone who can help you.

Question Time

If something happened to you and you needed help.
Do you think it is important to tell the whole story and that you are absolutely truthful in what you are saying about the other person that did something bad towards you, and why?

_____

_____

Never make a story up to get someone in trouble.
Always tell the truth, it does not matter how difficult it is.

No More Secrets Rule

Kids have lots of rules.
One rule that is important for kids to learn is the:
"No More Secrets Rule"

Rule 1. We should not have any secrets!

Rule 2. If somebody asks you to keep a secret we want you to learn to say: **"NO! I am not allowed to keep secrets. I will tell!"**

Rule 3. Surprises are **OKAY**!!! Surprises are things that get told pretty soon and usually make people happy.

Remember

- Your parents do care what happens at school. If you have a problem at school talk to your parents about it.
- If you have a problem at home, talk to your teachers about it or anybody else on your "**Let's Talk List**".
- If you have a problem and nobody is listening. Keep on telling people until somebody listens and helps you. If that does not help it is a good time to make use of the people on your IMPORTANT "Let's Talk List".
- If you don't tell anybody, nobody will know or understand what is going on and will be unable to help you.

Children's Rights

You have the right to:

1. Be treated fairly no matter what.
2. Have a say about decisions affecting you.
3. Live and grow up healthy.
4. Have people do what is best for you.
5. Know who you are and where you come from.
6. Believe what you want.
7. Privacy.
8. Find out information and express yourself.
9. Be safe no matter where you are.
10. Be cared for and have a home.
11. Education, play and cultural activities.
12. Help and protection if you need it.

Source: www.humanrights.gov.au/childrights
Australian Human Rights Commission

108   57

"Let's Make This World Happier"

Now that you worked through your Take-A-Stand Healthy Behaviour Development Child Workbook, you are officially invited to order your Bully Prevention Advocacy Pack!

Contact us to order your Advocacy Pack!

"Together we can make a difference."

azelene@kidzucate.com.au
www.kidzucate.com
0405 246 176

Take-A-Stand
Healthy Behaviours Development Program

The **Take-A-Stand Healthy Behaviours Development Program** *Teachers Manual, Advocacy Manual, Children's Workbook,* Electronic Program with *Video's* and *Online Program* were developed by Azelene Williams. This program is based on the original *Take-A-Stand Prevention of Bullying and Interpersonal Violence Program* and used with permission by Sherryll Kraizer, Ph.D.

All rights reserved. No part of this book may be reproduced or transmitted in any form or by any means whatsoever without express written permission from the author and program owner Azelene Williams, except in the case of brief quotations embodied in critical articles and reviews. Please refer all pertinent questions to the publisher.

www.kidzucate.com

azelene@kidzucate.com.au

Edited By: Alana Marshall

ISBN 978-0-646-96477-5

111 59